Tantra-zawadi's new collection is a must to read. It bubbles through every corner of the world. The symbolic bubble lofted in the air will leave many with multiple meanings of the beauty of life — a dose of inspiration — bringing the world closer to peace and hope.

I am permanently inspired by Tantra-zawadi. She is not only a poet — she is my hero. Let history not leave out those who remained on the ground inspiring communities and breaking taboos whilst at the same time uniting the global village. I fully endorse this book and I ask every human being in the world to bubble their lives with this amazing great piece of art.

— Betty Makoni, Founder of the Girl Child Network
and a 2009 Top Ten CNN Hero

Bubbles

ALSO BY TANTRA-ZAWADI

Gathered at Her Sky: Life Poems
Hoboken, NJ: Poets Wear Prada, 2010

alifepoeminprogress
New York: Chuma Spirit Books, 1999

Bubbles

One Conscious Breath

Tantra-zawadi

illustrated by

Edwin Boone

POETS WEAR PRADA • Hoboken, New Jersey

Bubbles

Poets Wear Prada
533 Bloomfield Street, Second Floor
Hoboken, New Jersey 07030
http://pwpbooks.blogspot.com

First North American Publication 2013
First Mass Market Paperback Edition 2013

Grateful acknowledgment is made to the following publications where some of these poems have appeared or are forthcoming:

Black Mermaids in Vision & Verse; a Poetically Spoken Anthology, Volume I; A Gathering of Words: Poetry and Commentary for Trayvon Martin; and "Rabbit Ears: An Anthology of Poems About Television."

ISBN-13: 978-0615819631
ISBN-10: 061581963X

Library of Congress Control Number: 2013909148

Printed in the U.S.A.

Front Cover Image: Oliver Covrett and Shanna Melton
Cover Author Photo: Jay Franco
Interior Author Photo: BymshaBrownePhotos@me.com
Interior Illustrator Photo: John Braithwaite
Coneria Script Font: Måns Grebäck

for

Africa

FOREWORD

Some would call Tantra-zawadi's creations "poetry," and her latest collection a "book of poems." But it's really a dare — a double-dare — to share a journey to the core of our individual and collective experience of love — love for ourselves and for our precious ever-evolving humanity.

From country music to pulp fiction, from pop songs to epic poetry, seems like we are all too ready for hearts-in-love to be broken, for dreams and visions to go unrealized. Tantra-zawadi's words, written and spoken, offer a different paradigm — a trail of hearts daring to be open.

Tony Vacca
World Music percussionist
Founding member of The Senegal-America Project
www.tonyvacca.com

TABLE OF CONTENTS

Foreword

Haiku:

Reflections of Africa	3
Senegal Morning	3
Home	3
Morning	3
The Dance	4
Wind	4
Rain	4
Seasons	4
Here	5
Woman	5
Flow	5
My Romantic Love	5
Adonis Cries	6
Towers	6
Strolling	6
Sea	6
Protective Love	7
Deepa	7
Real Self Calling	7
Warrior Woman	7
Four	8
Sleep	8
The Long Good-bye	8
Soon	8

In the Struggle 9

Troy Davis 9

Forgiveness 9

Marvin 9

Things Gotta Change 11

Radiator Grooves 14

Same Sanford 17

The Breakdown 20

Haiku:

Awash in Love 23

Recall 23

Steps 23

Only Now 23

Occupy Wall Street 24

Cherished Love 24

Help Coming Through 24

Night Calls 24

Divine 25

Reflections 25

Fine Lady 25

Escape 25

Pretty 26

Poetic Notion 31

Afro Waters 34

Jayne Cortez 36

Acknowledgments

About the Author

About the Illustrator

Bubbles

I carry dreams and romance of new fools and old flames
between the musk of fat
and the side pocket of my mink tongue.

— **JAYNE CORTEZ**

Reflections of Africa

Take me, take me home!
Across the wailing great blue
To the land of soul

Senegal Morning

Her sandy presence
Red sugar dust in the wind
African sunrise

Home

Her life is my tongue
Her wisdom is the embrace
Africa is home

Morning

Welcome like a breeze
Billowing my cotton skirt
In salutation

The Dance

Your words soft like rain
Fall beside my warmth and joy
Making language dance

Wind

She is fast and strong
Her branches tremble and bend
When she pours her dance

Rain

Eyes wide in wonder
Tongue outstretched to catch the rain
I am drenched in love

Seasons

Your kind of love leaves
Empty branches in the spring
Cherry blossoms fall

Here

Tears dry when love comes
They fall silent when love leaves
Eyes cry just the same

Woman

I am a woman
A creation of beauty
A movement of love

Flow

Remember the time
The river flowed easily
And our eyes took rest?

My Romantic Love

The romantic way
You hold me is like heaven
Romantic lover

Adonis Cries

Astounding beauty
In the art form of adore
Alas, you are man

Towers

I've seen worlds crumble
Felt the earth rumble beneath
Tumbled memories

Strolling

Time passes slowly
Blues from the streets sing my cries
Poems for water

Sea

The sun warms the sea
Becoming one with the air
For tomorrows' rains

Protective Love

Oh romantic one
Chase darkness into hiding
Shining in its face

Deepa

Fire burns deep inside
With him I am not falling
Deeper just the same

Real Self Calling

Honor your real self
The voice of inner-standing
Rising within you

Warrior Woman

I will not feign sleep
Nor will I sit in silence
Warrior woman

Four

The seasons know me
Remind me I am ocean
In waves and ripples

Sleep

Interesting how
Innocence yearns for slumber
When our bodies kiss

The Long Good-bye

Have you not a care
For the woman you embrace
Disappearing now

Soon

You know she will leave
You give her all of nothing
Playing with her heart

In the Struggle

The heart of a man
Knows the hearts of shackled men
Lost in the struggle

Troy Davis

What is true freedom?
How does man decide who lives?
I am Troy Davis

Forgiveness

Gentle is the place
Where the heart speaks openly
Oh, divine is forgiveness

Marvin

Scratching the rhythm
Vinyl dreams in rotation
Oh distant lover

THINGS GOTTA CHANGE

Young minds fertile and anxious
To deliver truth passed down
From griots with open minds
Prophesying from street corners, townships
And villages, about movements and phrases.
Finding ways to celebrate the rhythm of humanity
   and change.
Shattering glass with our third eye
For a clearer view of real love

How many dreams must die
For poems of life to rise?
Things, things gotta change

Although we struggle to survive
We thrive in clay, steel and concrete
Through the valleys, the deserts and homelands
Love provides and is sufficient
To grow soulful beings
Capable of letting go and letting live
Purpose being freedom we believe

For every man and woman
Every land and nation can join hands and
Lift their voices for a cause
Because some things gotta change

How many dreams must die
For poems of life to rise?

This is not a game
Real tears flow in real time
Real women becoming undone
Children raising themselves
Affected by infections of destruction
Cures strangled in economic strongholds
Accessibility denied so they dig more graves
And capture more slaves
As survivors simultaneously mobilize
For change because some things gotta

If we want to survive
How many dreams must die
For poems of life to rise?

Real men in real time

Warriors of love

Chanting down fear with instruments

Of power and light

For the fight is purely spiritual

Strong and long on courage

Awake to the foolishness and trickery

Mind focused on victory

Life poems healing and saving

The planet from anti-inhabitants by establishing

Letters of peace that calm the seas

Yes, we need to hug trees for real and

Break/fast without dropping bombs and shady deals that
   incite death

For the fight is purely spiritual

Our souls are at stake and baby

Things, things gotta change

RADIATOR GROOVES

Sitting by the window
Watching passersby
Radiator grooves
On the backs of my thighs

Memories of laughter from the concrete below
Jump rope chants of "Go sister, go"

Watching Daddy drive up
In his sky blue Belvedere
Lifting a shiny color television set high in the air
Wonders of Tinker Bell, Mr. Greenjeans and Captain
   Kangaroo
The box
Oftentimes entertaining
Mainly gave me the *blues*

Watching vibrant young men sent off to war
Wrestling images of who they were before

Sitting by the window

Watching passersby
Radiator grooves
On the backs of my thighs
I wondered
If there was a place for me behind all that glass
Overtaken by images of narrow escape
By the working class

Marches, funerals and heroes in black shoes
This brown-eyed girl preferred books
By poets spouting truth

Radiator grooves
On the backs of my thighs
Urban impressions forever on my mind
Through eyes both old and new
I see that television man
Is still flipping the *blues*

SAME SANFORD

A Poem for Trayvon Martin (1995 – 2012)

No resurrection for this kind of heavy
Sanford crossings run deep

Aches
Same as Jackson
Same as Omaha
Same as Memphis

Go on and sing the blues
The blues wrote the songs

Night stalkers
Up and downtown
Creep, creeping around
Quiet as justice
No fault to be found

Go on sister and sing the blues
The blues wrote the songs

Lawdy! Lawdy!
Justice slow dragging her feet
On streets of Skittles
Folks packing heat as
Another sun goes down

The beat goes on baby
The blues wrote the songs

What flows through Sanford's veins?
Another Memphis?
Another Money, Mississippi?

Folks goin' down real slow
Just like the blues
That wrote the songs

Sanford crossings run deep
Just like the blues
That wrote the songs

THE BREAKDOWN

I want to take my love back

Can you dig it?

Get it all back

Neatly wrap myself inside

A love-in of selfish egotistical appreciation

Without predispositions

Without prejudice

Without warm fuzzy feelings

Moaned against muffled promises in

Life-giving seconds of a tentative

I love you

Peppered with pet names

That is bound to change

And return again

Like a boomerang

Like time on a different day

But I can't

Take my love back

Hoard it

Get it all back

Without a breakdown

Confessing flesh-ordered infections

Of the mind, body and soul

Captivated by the inflection

By the jerking and the coming

The robotics of temporary involvement

Disguised as warmth and desire

Resulting in a lifetime of straight biology

Complicated in the giddiness of pheromones

Bare skin and scent

Struggling to hold on

To their need for simultaneous

Spiritual identification

I want to take my love back

Can you dig it?

Get it all back

Segue into sacred information

Connected to the psychology of the one who

Doesn't answer prayers with one-night stands

Or spiritual weapons

The one in the

Sunrise and the glass half full

The glimpse of potentiality

The lifeline

The medicine

The recovery

The first and twelfth step

The new dawn

The meltdown

The *get back*

The *take back*

The breakthrough

The shattering

The crystal

The life

The new feeling

The timeless

Awesome wonder of the

I am

Awash in Love

In the tub of love
There is truth and chemistry
Creating balance

Recall

Mindful of moments
Precious time given presence
Oh, sweet memories

Steps

Absence reminds us
Of the things we let go of
With eyes straight ahead

Only Now

When you embrace me
My whole being awakens
Into love's release

Occupy Wall Street

Standing in the square
Thoughts of freedom on your mind
Strong, bright and awake!

Cherished Love

The presence of heart
A sacrifice for a friend
Is the love you save

Help Coming Through

Love me with your words
Sing them with your heart and soul
Breathe me a poem

Night Calls

Cries in the silence
Carried on the wings of might
Call the warrior

Divine

So grateful for you
Your shining light upon me
Is all that I need

Reflections

Standing together
Facing the endless ocean
Returning to love

Fine Lady

May goodness find you
In the darkness of your thoughts
You will need her soon

Escape

Morning after rain
Unfurling like a heartbeat
Between life and death

PRETTY

I remember her so pretty
Pretty was her business
Updos
Press and curl
Nails painted red
Powder
Lipstick and
Mascara

Why they call it *makeup*?

When he met her
She was so pretty
Pretty was his business
Kissed her powdered face
Held her soft hands
Made himself up
To be her man

Why they call it *my man*?

When he took Pretty out

They looked so fly
When he twirled her around
She smiled real wide
Cheesin' was her business
Like sweet potatoes and fried chicken
He never left her side
So she made herself up
To be his woman for life

Why they call it *his woman*?

When he left
She was still pretty
But after he left
So did Pretty

She packed her pressing comb
In his traveling bag and
Lipstick kisses on
White shirts with all
The love she had
Fingernails chipped
From dialing

When he didn't answer the phone

She chain-smoked

Her business away

Unsmiling

She fell in love with her bottle

Pretty was no longer any of her business

Too risky

Too costly

Pretty now was cheap wine and whiskey
When she could afford it
No hair to be done
No lipstick to blot
No dresses to float in
No lover to adore her
She rarely bathed

Smoking and drinking
Smoking and stinking
Drinking and shrinking
She wore her slippers to the store
No one was looking for her
Pretty anymore

So she walked the streets
Talking to herself about
Her pressing comb in his
Traveling bag like it
Was her heartbeat

Heart broken like the bottles
About her bedroom

Quiet like the things he left

She eventually drank herself to death

And everyone tsked tsked and shook their heads

Because she used to be so pretty

With her fingernails painted red

Before she gave him her love

Why they call this *love?*

POETIC NOTION

A Poem for Laura Nyro (1947 – 1997)

Their voices
Trembled my troubles
Encouraged visions of a peaceful land
With clean water, food aplenty
Sweet music, lovemaking
Seasons of prosperity
And soulful gatherings
For the "Lonely Women" of the world

Their voices
Trembled my troubles
Blew them like a breeze into
Morning, noon and Goddess Twilight as
The woman by the window
Lit a flame and sang the blues
In keys of "Sweet Blindness"
Her "Wild World" now a satisfied blink

How quickly it all goes
The sun dances at twilight

Trouble rolls

Something in their voices
Called upon mothers whispering
Positive vibes for inclusion
In the Book of Life
Clinging to the lyrics of
"I Never Meant to Hurt You"
Between the self of knowing and
The self they wished to believe

"The Confession" called "Luckie"
Found its way into their voices
Hitting the highs and lows of "And When I Die"
Singing the blues out loud on the "Poverty Train"
Because they believed
In something

Something in their voices
Reminded me of why
Friends laugh through candles and
Birds night fly
The sun dances at twilight

Why you were the man

Because things are falling

Falling

Falling

As newspapers blow down the street

And pass you

Like brown leaves

How quickly it all goes

The sun dances at twilight

Trouble rolls

"Eli's Comin'"

"Stoney End"

AFRO WATERS

Many have dreamed
Of her magic
Her succulent hue
The power of her massive tail
Ebony skin beneath the blue

Bracelets on her mighty wrists
Bongos for waist beads
Music — her womanly core
She flirts with the stars
In search of her pleasure
Oh African mermaid of the waters
Buried in the hearts of men
Love is her treasure

Her voice calms the ocean
A comfort for the newly free
Rocking them to the door of their return
Destiny liberty
Oh African mermaid
A vision beyond earthly measure

Generous is her love

A sanctuary in the hearts of men

Oh! Sweet is her treasure

JAYNE CORTEZ

Poet/performance poet (1934 – 2012)

So glad she had Firespitters to ride her words

Move between her breaths

Sway when her mouth opened

Slide between her teeth with the passion

Of one who had lived

Every inch of every letter of every curve

Past every nail with the precision

To glimpse the sunrise in West Africa

Because she wanted them to

Stretch from New York City to the edges of the world

With handmade clothespins to grip moments

Urging people to see and create and discover

The sounds of their own voices, their thoughts

And push back against the tides of *they say* and *they do*

When all you supposed to do is be you

So glad she had Firespitters to ride her words

So she could breathe

Words that blasted and lasted and painted and scatted

And gave birth in the deepest shade of red

For every man, every woman, every African can

And so she wrote and wrote

Love notes across the sky in Harlem

And you can still hear her if you stand

Outside the Schomburg in the morning

Just because her voice dances there

And you would want to

You would want to

Hear the beauty in yourself

And taste the spirit of her language

Spit through the fire and into the burn of our hearts

Because she had Firespitters to ride with her

And I am so glad

I am so glad

That she did

That we all did

And we will someday meet in Senegal again

Because she would want us to see what we want to see:

The colors of words dancing free

ACKNOWLEDGMENTS

The author extends her thanks to the following publications where some of these poems have previously appeared or are forthcoming:

"Afro Waters"   *Black Mermaids in Vision & Verse*, edited by Torreah "Cookie" Washington, catalog for *Mermaids and Merwomen in Black Folklore: A Fiber Arts Exhibition*, City Gallery at Waterfront Park. Charleston, SC, August 2012

"The Breakdown"   CD *Sacred*, Tantra-zawadi Self-released: 2007, lifepoetry by Tantra-zawadi with music by Michael Cox

"Pretty"   *a Poetically Spoken Anthology, Volume I*, Inner Child Press: 2011

"Radiator Grooves"   "Rabbit Ears: An Anthology of Poems About Television," edited by Joel Allegretti, Poets Wear Prada: 2013

"Same Sanford"   *A Gathering of Words: Poetry and Commentary for Trayvon Martin*, Inner Child Press: May 2012

Practicing gratitude!

I thank God daily for all the people and places that have inspired this book of poetry. Without the blessing of life, creativity, family, friends and a brilliant team of supporters, none of this would have been possible. I cherish the experiences and relationships that have challenged my growth and opened my heart to love: especially my parents, Walter and Betty; my sons, Justin Jelani and Chuma Ayodele; my sister

Deb Williams; Tony Vacca and Massamba Diop (founders of The Senegal-America Project); Betty Makoni (founder of the Girl Child Network); the award-winning Senegalese singing group Bideew Bou Bess; Najee Dorsey (founder of Black Art in America); Nonradio Music; Shanna Melton, Edwin Boone, Bianca Dorsey, Stephanie Griffin, Abiodun Oyewole, Mwalim Peters, Adina Williams, Dana Byrd, Lupe, Karen Hunter, Espace Sobobade, Chuma Whahid Rasul, Precious Gift, Von Jacobs; the record labels and producers I work with for making words dance; the house music and poetry communities; and my publisher and production editor, Roxanne Hoffman and Jack Cooper, for believing in me and helping me bring this together.

You are a part of the story that I call love.

Peace and Love,

ABOUT THE AUTHOR

A work of *love* — what Tantra-zawadi makes — what she achieves through her art, envisioning, she says, the "unseen reality." A sublime soulfulness suffuses it, pungent like incense, subtle sinuous transformation shape-shifts as a genie might, rustled by a reedless wind. Its sizzle-cymbaled syzygy unites that, familiarly met, we thought we knew — blindness preceding a first kiss, bittersweet after — with a mastery of mood, trilled to transcendence, encouraging independence, womanly presence and voice, to embrace experience alongside others.

Comprehensive her exploration, with an awareness 360 and beyond, Tantra addresses the world and *its* poetry — poet to poet, enjoined in the present, evolving, through media, traditional and new, in print and performance, on the internet and off: visualizing word for the page, spoken on stage or before the camera, shaped to accompaniment by music — never diminished. Hers is a responsibility taken on behalf of others. Whom Brooklyn began enlivens a world; Tantra the artist is now sought and received.

She permits neither the page's edge nor the stage, the end of the music or the script to prescribe her method, limit her manner of engagement or define her role. Conjunction, for Tantra, succeeds through sum of dramatic parts. "Girl: A Choreospective" augmented *The Numeral Thr3ee* Off Broadway, "Soldier Blues," movement with words and music, further rite, to *A Night of Three Goddesses* at New York's Lincoln Center. "The Fear," contributed to *An Evolution of Reinvention*, "Stolen Dreams," like "Leaving My Apartment and Other Urban Adventures" — songs, too, inspiriting the Von Duvois Dance Collective — shared meaning in context of collaboration and combined effect. Her performances, at large, grace diverse stages, enthrall standing room in South Africa, London, Berlin, local museums, audiences on radio and TV.

Tantra's centrifugal perception, radial creativity and energy continually find wavelength to match her inventiveness and skill. She beats words into ploughshares. Love, conquering *all*, must still triumph over HIV and AIDS. Video of her poem "Scarlet Waters" assisted Product Red in emblazoning awareness. Tantra herself directed two short documentaries to that purpose: *Girl, the Film — Volume I, A Message from Ardija Red-Cloud* and *A Silent Genocide — A Brief Insight into HIV/AIDS*. "Girl" the poem received nomination for a Pushcart Prize in 2010; its author — mother in her own right and mentor for the Girl Child Network, partial beneficiary of the proceeds from her book sales — received the Kings County District Attorney's Office's Women's History Month Award in 2001 for her artistic contributions to the borough of Brooklyn.

She reminds us *root* portrays gestation of seed. *Tantra*, in Sanskrit, expressive of expanding consciousness; *zawadi*, Kiswahili, precious gift — metabolize a different speech, a new place, new times. Tantra comes and goes on spoken word, enters on "poem" both the building and *house*. She continues to work with Precious Gift, her point of original collaborative departure configured on the number three. *Love Planet*, released through Camio Recordings in 2008, traces Tantra's participation in Collective Spirits to the reissue, this year, by Do It Now Recordings (DIN) and distribution in South Africa. With Dana Byrd, collaborations — "Secret of Life," 2010 (Nev Records and DIN); "Don't Let It Go," 2010 (DIN); "2 Shades of Deep," 2011 (DIN); "We Are the Stars," 2012 (Gotta Keep Faith Recordings); "Change All Over Me," 2012 (Shines Records); "Guru Dance," 2013 (Uno Mas Recordings); and counting — number the DJs, Nastee Nev, SoulAgenda, Dolls Combers, Indy Soul, Steve Paradise, … Sunday mornings, midnight to 2 a.m., and again evenings, 7 to 8 p.m. (Central European Time), *One Love — One House* and *Shades of Love*, she shares the best in house music, disco, love songs, and more, as selector on Indamixworldwide.

Prominent in periodical, widely anthologized, Tantra-zawadi returns to print, book three in hand — its forerunner, *Gathered at Her Sky: Life Poems*, also from Poets Wear Prada (2010), successor to her debut *alifepoeminprogress* (Chuma Spirit Books, 1999).

ABOUT THE ILLUSTRATOR

Boston-born African American, Edwin Boone — early introduced to visual art, attending the Elma Lewis School of Fine Arts (later, to become the National Center of Afro-American Artists) in the early nineteen seventies — gravitated to an empirical one, its meditation painstaking rendering of the given and tangible, its concept perception proved through precision, a balance achieved, vision indivisible from a clarity of that viewed. Inspired by academic tradition — paths leading from France, classicism, the first (and prototypical) "neo"; Italy, Russian impressionism, social realism — Edwin extends its scope, media, techniques, and values prized to include visualization of the African American experience. His training and immersion touch New York landmarks of the "Atelier Method": the Bridgeview School of Fine Art, National and Grand Central academies, Art Students League; most recently, Atelier Armetta, at the Long Island Academy of Fine Art in Glen Cove.

© John Braithwaite 2013

He seeks to share "emotional experience ... meaningful ... lasting images ... clearly understood without interpretation." Beauty, he writes — "found" — avails opportunity "to create the closest thing to paradise on Earth."

Edwin founded the African American Realist Society in July

2011. This year [2013] New York's chapter of the National Conference of Artists, the country's oldest, largest cultural organization supporting Black art, elected him president.

www.ingramcontent.com/pod-product-compliance
Lightning Source LLC
Chambersburg PA
CBHW060202070426
42447CB00033B/2290